THE RETURN
OF THE NATIVE

KATE COLBY

UGLY DUCKLNG PRESSE

The Return of the Native
© Kate Colby, 2011

First Edition, Ugly Duckling Presse, 2011
ISBN 978-1-933254-77-7

Library of Congress Cataloging-in-Publication Data

Colby, Kate.
  The return of the native / Kate Colby. — 1st ed.
     p. cm.
  ISBN 978-1-933254-77-7 (pbk. : alk. paper)
  I. Title.
  PS3603.O419R47 2011
  811'.6—dc22

                                        2010051410

Ugly Duckling Presse
at the Old American Can Factory
232 Third Street, E002
Brooklyn, NY 11215
(www.uglyducklingpresse.org)

Distributed by Small Press Distribution
(www.spdbooks.org)

Ugly Duckling Presse is a member of the
Council of Literary Magazines and Presses.

Design & Typesetting: Don't Look Now!
Type: Gloucester, Gill Sans, Garamond
Cover Printing: Ugly Duckling Presse
Cover Paper: Fabriano / Tiziano
Printing & Binding: McNaughton & Gunn

Thank you to the editors of *Coconut, NO: A Journal of the Arts*
and *Shampoo,* in which sections of this poem first appeared.

KATE COLBY

THE RETURN OF THE NATIVE

TABLE OF CONTENTS

I don't ever want to see this world again—not with these eyes.

—LALITA MADHAVA DAS

The Inevitable Movement Onward

So, he laid down his hammer and he died.

A world is peopled with Xs for eyes

    and gotten away

    with toll taken late
    and just as soon
    assigned to last year's
    bottom line.

Pioneer Days one pays
to pan for gold—fool's
nostalgic pay dirt
trumps being played

    triplets with your left hand
        two-timing with your right.

Sky-high and hand-tying
green's fee of the strapped
ways and means overseeing trustees

    a yonder
    that's rather
    more yellow

    let mellow
    if anything other
    than fangled.

Plucked from rolling pie-cart at the roll call—

        to want
        to take
        this role
        and fill it

say throwing Wessex back on the wheel
so the product becomes its packaging.

The Morning and the Evening of a Day

Slowly grows
the hoary morn
of fingered frost
infection spread
across the wavy windows.

      A fingerprint burns
      in reflexive research
      for identical snowflakes,
      the invisible seam of this
      sugar-egg landscape

      before it clouds over

again with sanded banks
and frozen ruts in the mud

a dampened thud
on the slumping
stoop

a bit of movement
in the bowels of the morning's
historical romance

say something starring Depardieu.

My non-dairy creamer
is clumping your coffee

my coffee-
mate clouding your cup o'
my coffee

(adopted   (abandoned
highway   right blinker

          blinking

and the sky is as round as the rest of it.

The grist mill ground
away with the water
source dried
up pipes
jazzy track at the Post Road Payless—

Hey Jude,
you're chipping away
that stone dust in your nose
isn't really real, but at least
you can feel it.

I'd like to be at home
in a truck backing up
in the morning, the sound

of salt on the road,
the bottle rolling
around in the back

to have like lichen
reciprocal sense of my own

functional duck boots,
bug juice, boiled dinner

			—wouldn't mind at all
my mind running off at the mouth
while things crust up in its corners.

Is it geodesy or stick-to-itive
local parsimony, my practical
Congregational education
in always putting to good use

the drippings.

This old thing?

A stopper chain
rust stained, so

strip it.

In decline
an ancient line
of
		rethinking

		better leave it
		in the mud room.

Firmness Is Discovered in a Gentle Heart

And just for the record
this is not jazz but light
over the lip of the black
hole—suction required
to stick to the side,
a centrifugal ride

        The Gravitron
        —Turkish Twist?

the fist
I will shatter
in this unblinking mirror.

Rough Coercion Is Employed

Cart has overtaken horse
and is now overturning

      trot trot to trot trot

It's all downhill from here.

Things that didn't antecede
their names
were made and meant
to be made ready

      all colors already
      discovered, a county
      of traces on wayside signposts.

A taste of fame and of a sudden
all those years suck down the drain
in retroactive assignation

      in a role like a ring
      too big for the finger

         as slipped on retro-spected,
         checkered past and kinged
         by retracting escape ladder

         climb up into a narrow window
         and draw the blinds behind you.

Trees on tiny offshore islands
with theoretical leaves

and all the things that can't happen
simply because you know they can't.

    The sky is white
    with the kind of lightning
    that always strikes at least twice
    and hail the size of the holes
    in your windshield—stopping   you dead
                            your tracks

    wrapped in a paper bag
    with tax-free rocks and salty rims
    at the wayside Stateline Liquor Store.

    [We will not be undersold!]

How a life
takes on a life
its very own.

Can't resist one last
round on the house
and every single time.

Sharp Words Are Spoken and a Crisis Ensues

History loves company.
Old soldiers lie
only six inches under.
Spoon up next to them
in two-player games of
sardines—turn the key
and close the can behind me.

        Keep your distance; I am
        the sound of a rock or raft
        around which water laps

        bubbles in hard candy
        that cut your tongue
        and make your candy
        taste like blood

        a plastic Adirondack chair.

        I've beeped back up into
        stomping grounds: boot-
        scrapes, stoops
        I've tracked all over the house

                have to cough
                just to feel
                my own soft
                interior walls

buzzing with darkness
and wheezy insects
soughing in the trees
peters out pre-dawn
and into the hollow
feeling of fall.

    Sleepy seeds crusting
    the corners of my eyes

        dusk breaks scarlet
        sumac, bayberry,
        bittersweet scent of
        my waxy wick:
        Autumn Mist

           a security blanket
           to bleed out into.

To write only to have
thought of something
(or the opposite)

an empty packet of sweetener
(in case of emergency)

My dead are where my lands lie buried

between the Hilltop Steakhouse and Suffolk Downs

        and never to regain
        the ground
        we've turned into.

A Desperate Attempt at Persuasion

To move
so to see
the medium
in a moment.

Home is where
the head is
taken.

       Lying back in a warm bath
       waiting for the water
       to get cold in a gradual
       disambiguation—

       dear amphibian,
       never mind the slow death,
       only jump at the sudden.

Now back in the technicolonial
color of my youth—bitter blue
juniper berries
crushed between fingers

lackluster pewter,
umbrella tines, rusted
tins of powder
Colman's Mustard.

A frowsy form at the bitter end
of cross-continental continuum—
power lines and cloud formations

Harley Ds and E Clampus Vitus
chapter saloons, bee-stung barmaids
in fin-de-siècle-reminiscent pantaloons

slapped-on bumper regalia
of entitlement: supporting our troops
on a run for a roll of electrical tape

[You break it, you buy it.]

[Check your alignment.]

—screaming big rigs—

[How's my driving?]

to the Winnemucca Flying J.

Over title I'd take the chain on my stopper,
my own corroding string of beads and couplings
and what goes out with the bathwater.

Were I to reside in a sugar egg,
snow-white landscape of pure analogy

shiny schist sidewalks
with adhesive safety
of slip-proof daisies.

Uh oh, non-dairy overload—
put your face in and blow

bubbles for your own
time
being;
holding your breath is not
the same as not breathing.

My epistemological pace car
lapping me—
give a vigorous scissor kick,
touch my finger to the mirror

to live within
a finger-licking inch
of your own life

(but don't fall in!)

Now I'm just dating myself.

Humanity Appears upon the Scene, Hand in Hand with Trouble

All is safely gathered in

      stone walls will wind
      around and through it

      drained veins
      one man's hands
      his own land
      effaced and lichened
      ways of life.

Such description
the instant written
turns to bone, bleached
skeleton—any story
is as real as that
which swings in its stand
in the examination room

         nervous
         tissue
         paper
         light

[If you lived here you'd be home right now.]

When who's there lands before the knock

                    then prick your finger
                    just so you can
                    suck on it.

I've seen my own murmuring heart
being monitored

          the skip
          in my signature's
          dotted line.

(Hurling my plates at the wall—

                    the pain-
                    precluding
                    drip, breathing

                    deep unlearned
                    in circular
                    surface aspiration

                    You won't feel a thing.

I'll eat with my goddamn hands!)

          A man
          ain't nothin' but a man

tooth and nail.

A Conjuncture, and Its Result upon the Pedestrian

Foggy haloes fade
      into day
      breaking
      into dark

      a broken
      silence is
      whirring.

      Were pudding to sputter
      at the end of a poker,
      were woodlanders wooding,
      would be so sweet without

my downwardly mobile window.

Some things pre-exist their purposes:

prefab vernacular architecture,
universally unflattering fashions,
interiors designed before ground
broken, insulation blown.

      (I'm taping syntactic
      paint chips to the wall

      my tonal continua that leave a lot
      to be determined by the color wheel.)

But a barn is nothing but a barn
is nothing if not site-
specific—around it cows
lie down for coming rain

       at the Little House on the Prairie House
       the Future Farmers of Everything

       leave a greasy patch on the Plexiglass,
       scratch-ticket ritual of local entitlement

       to the wheezy harmonica
       dragging down the highway—
       hangdog soundtrack
       of second generation
       twice removed
       from layers of the land

       and the kinds of things contained in silos:
       supposed wheat and the world's undoing

              a man-made winter
              stirring in your cup,
              my deliquescing pot

              my slurring serial signage screaming

              [This Space Available]

Pretty, pretty porcelain Tom
who's not whitewashing
the pickets and why, all
fill-in-the-blank as can be

milk-fed and creamy-
thighed, sleepy pie-
eyed sweetie,
time and edition
limited American
heritage figurine.

I can make of you
everything you are,
everything I need
to say is seared in
lazy cattle brands

Old West pan and pickaxe,
stocks, speckled pots,
painted ladies, fringy lampshades

      identity's event horizon
      ingesting everything
      that falls within an inch of my life

      whither my body
      meet my body
      coming through the wry.

A Lurid Light Breaks In upon a Darkened Understanding

This time you've been provided with a playbill:

>John Henry is the Strings
>Jude is the Bassoon
>This evening Jude will be played by the Flute
>The Wolf is the Contemporary
>The Hammer is the Strings
>This evening John will be playing the Strings
>The Drill is Non-Dairy is the Wessex is the Horns
>The Murmur is the Bird, the Flute
>The Bird is the Bassoon
>The Clarinet is the Reservoir (not yet formally introduced)
>The Triangle plays the Grist Mill is the *Ping* in the procession
>The Strings are the Strings and are writing the score
>Who is the Jazz? (There is no jazz.)
>The Strings are Jack and Tom and also me
>The Stopper plays Tambourine, rattles its Chain
>The Bass is the Hum and the Halo and the Wolf
>>and the hole
>>and the drain
>>and my home
>>the metronome
>>the native trope
>The West is the West is the Egg plays Sue is the Bassoon
>Hi, I'm Sue. I play the Bassoon.
>And that's History on the Oboe, wailing
>What don't mean a thing
>goo goo ga joob

She Goes Out to Battle Against Depression

Hey Sue
you're decamping
and hey, me
too, I'm in it
for a more innocent time.

Lost ground is gathered
and clumsily bundled
in the gloaming—then

        there was space
        and I was in it.
        Now I'm a blind bat rebounding
        from every over there where
        I have or haven't been.

To return in time for rutting season—
distant wincing cracks
dampened by velvet nap,
the tinkle of felt-covered
hammers hammers
over the murmur of my valves

    time is innocent, it's me
    that's merely aspirational

    a gasping pod
    beached on progress

    red shell cracked,
    dead feelers—no,

dead red roe
of delicacies-in-the-rough

netted: the sea

and what gives in too easily,
like institutional toilet tissue

I only want you
just so and that repeatedly
we fall down bent and kissing.

To be a ranch hand
scratching at the land
trampling the sage
sweet smell of
not right now

receiver of calling
and response,
a comfortable pew

> *and with you*
> *and with you*
> *and also with you*

this is how we gather together.

This is God's country, made
of molehills made of mountains
and what takes root with rail towns,
unquestionable stops along the way

wheat from chaff
curd from whey

distinctions reflected in hay-
gathering methodologies,
whether stacked, rolled or baled—

those things in the world called "otherworldly"
and the frequency with which they are found—

        at last I've got you, but now
        you're breaking up

        bellied-up to a bottomless
        pint of pick-your-own berries.

I am your dollop of non-dairy topping,
pie-faced Kilroy
peering backwards over a wall
watching our wake
wonder what it means
to have been
or to wish
to have been
was here.

A Face on Which Time Makes But Little Impression

The terminal annual Independence parade
gathers at the grange,
kicks off with a half-staff flag-raising.

An empty resonant *ping* against pole
in time
to memories made
dead (feel my bones)
before they're even formed, fossilized

or written in stone, stiles
are wiped clear from the map,
backtracking dotted lines
through every blooming pasture.

        Head soft with nostalgic
        construct, a thin-skinned
        fontanel fusing—

Finally, only walls
will remain to arrange
an inland sea of fluoridation
to reinforce the teeth.

Fleshy water lilies
entangle the ankles,
give a pleasing, plastic-y
slap to the surface.

But close your eyes and visualize
how birds will fare at the wind farm

uplifting flurry
of blade to wing.

Bunting undulates down Main Street.

A disincorporated town
prepares to be drowned
in the breeches of forebears
worn
with the spun drag of yesteryear.

The ever-embattled mill around

      one. two.
      stop. plant
      feet. jam
      butts into one
      last twenty-
      one gun salute

Smoke curls as through teeth,
billows in beds of bulging
lilies, velvet pistils
thrust and staining
petticoats of Prescott ladies.

Time has come, now
honor your partner,
complete the square
and prepare for the reel—

forward and turn
with the right hand round
an endless canon of shifting grounds.

[If you lived here you'd be home by now.]

What's been laid to rest is being amended,
all premonitory frissons rendered false

the hollow clack of skeletons
Eskimo kissing with their cavities

perennial daisies push up ditches,
expired petals over-arching

in the understory
of the forest, fiddleheads
unfurl though dank, dead leaves

(where my undead would lie buried).

A reel as seen through
windows, cold night
air remembers
me to my bones
my head to the snow
the silence on my radi-

o my flimsy castle made of candles
with said longevity of spermaceti

my stopper chain made
of smocking, chicken
salad.

        You say you prefer to take
        your fiddle with a little more squeak

        but I wouldn't come to your house
        and put my dirty feet all over the furniture.

Through the Moonlight

Let us always be about
to be leaving
one another for the evening

uncurl my fingers and kiss
the center of my palm

feel the chemistry

I bleed so you can
see yourself in it.

Slowly rowing
through water
lilies, a lady
reclined at the end
of a better century

begging you, please
don't rain on my tracing paper.

Living in cities,
architectural moments
when you become the space
that the body contains
—feel the physics—
and shrink with me
under my para-
pluie of bent tines.

I'd like to be the hairdryer
trained on the pipes
in the freezing ceiling of your cellar

to go ahead and sell the substance
even if the shadow isn't budging.

Sluggish bees in late season
suckle empty soda cans.

The Two Stand Face to Face

You've heard the horror stories
about swimming in quarries

at night, floating in the deep,
cold water on your back

hear the dead smell, in waves
cracking at Haul-About Point.

Chisel chinks in the granite,
small shrieks of steel on stone

the Pleiades is a fist, unclenching,
their bodies are never found.

Queen of Night

On some hallows' eve,
a hollow half-light,
the last of the leaves
in umber clumps
on fistular trees.

Anterior sinus spectra
of caraway, clove and wintergreen—
fumous memories
at the tips of desensitized tongues.

My recurrent yearning for the tried and true
old-fashioned confections
more easily reducible to category of "food":
rum balls, ribbon candy,
my second emblematic ice-box cake.

I am a record, not broken,
just needing its needle;
a dog, forever circling
the space I plan to occupy.

And away we go, hounding
the scent of woods (whose
woods?) through wide-eyed wood
and what we believe is a glade,
to the burial ground by the name
of the number on the stake.

With charcoal and tracing paper
we rub against the graves

all Smiths and Bishops
before the inscription
is effaced by another
hundred winters.

      Can't see past
      my own traced
      turkey hand

      throbbing embers

      woo woo pheasant feathers.

As lichen grows
only on the north sides of trees
I think I know
an arrowhead
from a common stone   chinks, steam
                                           drills scream

                                           but bloody light still
                                         gets in around the fingers.

In your old English
furniture finish
still stars move
much faster than you

cast no shadows
it is always noon

in the basement
of the natural
history museum.

We are staging a fight
with chalked sticks
where I would get
or be gotten to
in a dusty blue
ring stabbed gently
around the heart.

The Dishonesty of an Honest Woman

In the half-light of the entr'acte,
a synopsis and historical context:

>   a long walk
>   on a short
>   fourth wall

>   virtual coins behind virtual ears

>   better hock that ring
>   and live with it.

Beneath the reflective surface,
I am breathing through a hollow reed

>   dancing with the mic stand
>   squealing the needle

>   on the side of the sewing
>   you don't see

>   where the work happens.

My crafty sampler of secretly
discontinuous, tied-off threads

>   poor relations
>   claiming kin

the linchpin of my lexy cotton gin.

Trophy wives
with younger, better-looking husbands

Rochambeaux
of equally impotent elements

magic cups
upended over nothing.

We are formula-fed babies
with breath stolen by our own
cradle-capped contemporaries

buddy breathing
mist on the mirror

the sound of the metal ball rolling
at the bottom of the paint can.

So, please help yourself
to more of my zero-sum foodstuffs:
fatback, hardtack, pepperpot—do the math

net-net-net negative.

What hath my golden calf wrought?

unimproved means
unimproved end

just think
what with
your pretty face

a piece of work
maybe lace
works either way

figures.
curtains.

The Custom of the Country

An Indian giver of borrowed time
(would that I could undo the idiom)

or on winter mornings
heat rises in the nave,
stirs the devotional hangings.

Lick the spoon then redo the math—

> what our maker doth
> guarantee: death
> and mnemonic taxonomy

> and at a price
> that's hard to beat.

King Philip Called On Forty Girls Singing

> Whose King Philip?

> Whose thin crust?

> Whose worthless wampum
> under whose cup?

Chief Sachem Construction Paper Quiver

> some shadows are shaped
> like people.

In sum, I am one
of the many
desiccated ends of
things in the crisper

        would-be home-bound foundling

        with a cornerstone supporting
        umpteen other houses

        and the brighter the light
        the deeper the shadow

(someone has peed on the seat).

Methods of momentary marking
in Uberville: buying titles,
lunar real estate, in situ citation

        *Go thou my incense
        upward from this hearth—*

        learn to layer,
        let out hem,
        wick from the wax
        jack, live with it.

        Learn to like it:
        eating snow,
        taste of space,
        empty uncaloric
        ice-cream headache.

The fifth caller will receive
the reason for which he's calling

everything which has happened.

    (Wide unclasp the tables of their thoughts—)

    Unhasp the casement, drop your locks
    from an embattled tower of self-
    reflexive psychobabble

    save yourself, chase
    your own ambulance

    with your hand draw your hand
    and vice-versa and shake—

    I am my own spit sister,
    as Frankenstein is often
    confused with his monster

    The wind, indeed, seemed made for the scene
    as the scene seemed made for the hour.

Every Good Boy Deserves

    a bigger piece of the piano bench—
    roll up those sleeves and get into it.

What a girl is made of:

      lunchmeat, Fudgesicles,
      Sanka with sweetener,
      non-dairy creamer

      the frangible gum
      that comes with your trading cards.

When all is said, done, and DIY is not enough

      there are rows of backs
      of heads, flickering

            Another pearl for my string
            of what gets in
            under my skin
            surrounded with secretion—
            rub it
            till it
            begins to glow
            an old moon
            everyone's already seen,
            but searches for
            themselves in,
            anyway.

My Mind to Me a Kingdom Is

These same thoughts people this little world.

Eustacia Dresses Herself on a Black Morning

On top of the wold,
above fires expiring
in quavering embers,
commemorative cinders,
snuffed out by their own
attendant gently
settling
soot.

Jagged digits finger
in from the periphery,
freezing ponds, panes,
the eye
        of evergreen
        needles, crackling Sterno,
        expectant chafing dishes.

        We gather together
        in hot spots, cold places
        get even colder, we are
        suction countering suction,
        the sound of the finger sliding
        between chords, the sound
        of falling snow.

        The self-same flakes
        make sounds of scissors
        snapping at random
        but always the same

rap of the knocker   muffled

mummers mumming

    ringing ringing
    the sixth caller
    will not hang up
    empty-handed

I demand my consolation prize!

my pocket full of proverbial rye

      for the birds
      some dumb joke
      I don't even get
      but I'll take it
      so long as it
      once meant something

      for a song
      a skeleton
      tee-shirt.

This microphone makes waves,
ear-popping Eustachian sensation

    (tap tap. can you
    hear me now?)

Tracks played backwards
and what you hear there.

[Bridge Freezes
CAUTION
Before Road]

Put your face right up next to the globe

see unwound cassette tape
snakes along the sidewalk,
the frozen grass is glittering
with forever silent sonic code

contaminants you'd rather
keep out of your sources

[Beginning No Salt Zone]

The walls wind up
from the reservoir to the road,
continue on the other side.
A jack-knifed trailer.
Everybody's died.

        So, turn it over and shake,
        now everybody
        rehash the blizzard of '78—

        it seems this rag is meant
        for drier eyes than mine.

The Nth annual follies unfold
with ribbons a-flutter, another
dragon slain, princess saved.

(Pete's pulled the stopper
shoved the threat down the drain.)

Tikki Tikki Tembo
is drowning in the well

Wee Willie Winkie
in his moth-eaten nightgown

Jack Sprat's dead wife
leaves the world
only half-digestible.

And who's the lass behind the mask?

    Hi, it's just me,
    my own girl-next-door

    we respectively see
    redskins, reddlemen, same difference—
    same rosy x-ray vision. Look Peter,

        locking the wolf away
        locking yourself away

        either way, you're stuck, splayed
        like a gnat in the paint
        on the Don't-Fence-Me-In Fence

        a cardboard coffee tray
        and a dozen Munchkins

what you see
depends on the speed of your wipers.

They're turning on one another in the chase,
with a great defensive shedding of antlers

indifferent to the poachers
who've repaired the White Hart, anyway,
to put away

approximated food
you can eat forever—
hydrogenated cottage pie,
chicken fingers, curly fries.

In the end, everybody dies,
everybody's resurrected
year over year

while I'm down here
at the bottom of the well, watching
the bucket bang back up without me.

Echoing sound
of Soupy: come 'n'

git it, get up, shut up
and eat your dinner, young lady—

break bread, jam
hand down throat

and reexamine
the willfully indigestible.

We gather together
on a carpet of historic patterns,
a Greek key, half doubling back
on itself,
swastika and hound's-tooth.

I'll edge up next to the hearth,
climb right inside the screen
and look back out at you

through diamond-shaped panes

what is written on the wind:
nostalgie de la boue,
an ethereal plastic sack   whispering

                              thank you
                                    thank you
                                          thank you

You will eat what I put in front of you.

In new-fallen snow
the objects below
headstones like teeth
making it digestible.

I think I know
my own reflection
watch my head
fill up with snow.

Squinting through freezing windshield,
the wipers define the field—
this squeaky container
with this noxious blue
fluid, I am
quietly taking over the world.

A Coalition Between Beauty and Oddness

In winter, walls fade
up into woods
and the reel runs backwards.

Indian corn, rows of rotten
teeth, dendritic trees reach
out fruitlessly, cast no shade,
the lichen has a field day
in the cold, hard light.

Exhaust curls like dirty cream
from muffled tailpipes.

Riding in the way-back,
an extra-retrospective
advantage of vanishing
point being behind you.

At the end of the day
at the edge of our head-lit halo
restless specters curl from their graves

       backlit mist
       looks like rain

       the mind makes up
       most of it, anyway.

It's just another manmade
day on the road,
a piecemeal food pyramid
of cream-like injected centers,
numbered colors, x-plus-one
bottles of beer.

There are birds up there (began to sing).

The world is so much older here.

I'm all dolled up in my foul-weather gear,
searching the palm of my hand for a gale

take preventive measures of motion

sickness: a steady eye
                on the wavy horizon   slack flag
                                                           impotent spinnaker
                                                           stupid whirligig—

How many ships would this face sink?

depends on the relative
emptiness of the hold

on the volume of what
will flush into its own

with the purported coriolis
effects of your powder room.

Always swim parallel to the shore

and try to forget
everybody knows

there's a hole in the bottom of the sea.

The Figure Against the Sky

My airy osteo-
porous bones

a bird, a shell
contain the sea
or the sound of it

and the kind of cataracts
you can see through.

On the other side
of Dead Man's Curve
a word
whose non-existence
ruins all the others.

The chevron-shaped wings of frigates

the back of your hospital gown

flapping

>   on the line
>   in the wind
>   my skin is
>   shaped
>   like tee-shirts.

Perplexity Among Honest People

The good people of Prescott
will not take this standing up,
hold repeated town meetings
in chairs
affixed to the floor like theater seats

stripped of leaves, the tapped
trees are indistinguishable.

Things run backwards: taps
is played at the disinterment

when bodies are borne
teeth rattling like desiccated leaves
to the site of the future
redemption center.

The retractable map is rolled, packed
into a layer of civilized sediment

      a parfait
      a trifle
      a pancake breakfast
      a self-storage
      national treasure.

They plant rows of
butts on barstools,
can't go home,
so go to seed

weeds, creaky digits
finger in through the
cracks in the cobbles

their doubling dice are counter-weighted

another yellow stain pervades
the yellowed tavern wallpaper.

In a last unplanned Parade of Horribles
they set their spokeless wheels to the ruts

as the bubbles that cling
to the sides of your cup
give themselves over
one after one, they are

born-again babies,
new bodies to which
their very own names
haven't yet clung.

(Endow a star in my name,
stick another feather in my headdress:
co-opted macaroni,
American Chop Suey.)

From the air you see roads,
from the woods, the walls,
the crumbling foundations

sensation of teeth
in your mouth

the slop in the saucer

the sound of sparrows
smacking into glass

the faceted plastic fluorescent covers
in the basements of faded institutions.

We circulate in closed systems
of common tracks and breathe
the hand-me-down air with pink
plastic sacs from Chinatown—
our rattling, insufflating lungs,
our last-ditch divisor by which
we have gathered here together.

Say sister, can you spare
some air? Our gasping
lips kiss the ceiling

conducting signals
with our cavities,
our rotten fillings

strangers tuck tags
back into our shirts

(the tiny curls and knots at the nape…)

Just shut up and nobody gets hurt.

You are not who you think
and it's critical that we apply
the right name to the principle.

>   *Tutoyer* me,
>   slam your dice on the bar
>
>   just who do you think you are,
>   John, Tess, King Philip?
>
>   I become my milky stockings
>   at every April's Cerealia,
>   a pole dance for May Day—
>
>   do you read me?

I'll endow a chair
with my not-taken married name
then sit in it.

Baling wire. With barbs.
Things by way of which
we gather or are snared,
the harder you struggle
the more entangled you are

my syntax sucks
like quicksand

a risk-averse, televised
Guy Fawkes bonfire.

You are all going
to have to come
with me, please,
scrape your soles
before entering.

Mind the threshold
and the doorstop
and the slackened
weather stripping.

Welcome to my humble
mudroom *maquiladora*
where I in-source my labor

another offshore home
I build for myself
inside of the world

drowning where
my reflection used to be

where I dress
and redress
myself for dinner.

Those Who Are Found Where There Is Said to Be Nobody

Settle in for the winter
of our disconnect—
lips cracking, cheeks packed
with packing peanuts,
moth balls, walls of cedar.

Go home to papa, Peter;
the place is erupting
with pustular fungus,
little deaths of used-up leaves

        believe
        you
        me

Rabbit is asleep.

So, never mind the corkage fee,
things afforded by technology.

We draw in from the periphery
like slugs to beer,
the sky is so much closer here.

I'm Little Devil Doubt
running with an egg
in a silver-plated spoon

lying through the nose-
bleed section of history

[Please wipe down machines after use.]

I apply my squeegee
to the fog-free mirror

haven't seen you in forever

                          strains of
                          the recessional—

flush the pipes,
retire the greens keeper,
scrape the windshield

look alive, people

the arch should peak above the pupil.

An Old Move Inadvertently Repeated

Here, take it. You can have it.
The embroidery hoop
outside of which I work,
darn everything
for want of larger holes.

Backed up against
a bundling board
of increasing proportions

grinding my teeth and
kicking off the covers,
shallow sleep of being
not marriage material.

To climb inside the vitrine,
gather together the glass
flowers I want to break
between my teeth, hear
shatter in my head—

How will it end?
With neither a bang nor a whimper
but a weary,
insistent
banging.

Three cheers for Mrs. Bradford—

She fell over the side and died.
She fell back over the side and died.
She leaned back over the side and died.

You gave us quite a scare.

I return as Martin Guerre.

My tiny plot
I hoe and harrow
again and again
to see each time
what I might grow there.

The First Act in a Timeworn Drama

I will die with this hammer in my hand.

Making drip castles of sand

       one. two.
       one. two.

       if you can't see
       my mirrors
       can't see you

this is just another test of the system.

Now who do you think you are,
Tom—foolhardy, predatory
lender of reflective emergency blankets

while I root around
in coin returns, collecting
the off-shot of others'
cut-off conversations

I see through you

take a hammer to
what I presumed
was a hollow figure
only to discover
the creamy center.

I am only the projector
on which the plastic
transparencies are stacked

forever seated at the kids' table
with a broken elastic party hat

at an ongoing Annunciation
with the figure coming in
frontways from the side

> not abiding
> the rules of the rest

> forever fail my road test

> [Blind Drive Ahead]

> borne again all over again.

Whether Lent or Advent
the crèche is set up
the calendar's windows
opened onto sweetmeats
of a much bigger picture
that never coalesces
but returns every year
a little frayed, yet serviceable.

10 Italicized line adapted from a statement attributed to Sioux Chief Crazy Horse: "My lands are where my dead lie buried."

 The Hilltop Steakhouse and Suffolk Downs are a kitschy restaurant and a dog racing track located in Saugus and East Boston, Mass., respectively. Both are prominent landmarks on Boston's Route 1. Between them one passes through Melrose, Mass., which is home to the Colby family cemetery. I've never been there, but since I was a kid, have always pictured my elders buried behind the enormous illuminated green cactus at the Hilltop.

23 Prescott was a small town in central Massachusetts that was dissolved along with three others in 1938 when the Swift River Valley was drowned to create the Quabbin Reservoir, which is the primary water source for the city of Boston. The buildings were razed, the cemeteries relocated and the towns' inhabitants required to disperse with little or no assistance. Today, remnants of roads, walls and cellars can be seen from the air or when the water level is low.

28   "I sell the shadow to support the substance."
          —Sojourner Truth

37   Italicized lines from *Walden*, Henry David
          Thoreau, 1854.

38   "The wind, indeed..." from *The Return of the
          Native*, Thomas Hardy, 1878.

38, 40   "Wide unclasp the tables of their thoughts,"
          Troilus and Cressida, IV, v; "These same thoughts
          people this little world," *Richard II*, V, v. These
          quotations appear on a pair of stained-glass
          windows in the home of Sarah Winchester
          (1839-1922), heir to the Winchester rifle
          fortune, in San Jose, California.

59-60   Soon after arriving in the New World, William
          Bradford's wife, Dorothy, fell from the deck of
          the Mayflower and drowned.